ENDANGERED ANIMALS

Published by Creative Education, Inc., 123 South Broad Street, Mankato, Minnesota 56001

Printed by permission of Wildlife Education, Ltd.

ISBN 0-88682-269-6

ENDANGERED ANIMALS

Created and Written by
John Bonnett Wexo

Zoological Consultant
Charles R. Schroeder, D.V.M.
Director Emeritus
San Diego Zoo &
San Diego Wild Animal Park

Scientific Consultant
Kurt Benirschke, M.D.
Director of Research
San Diego Zoo &
San Diego Wild Animal Park

Creative Education

Art Credits

Pages Six and Seven: John Dawson: **Pages Eight and Nine:** Karl Edwards; **Pages Ten and Eleven:** John Dawson; **Pages Twelve and Thirteen:** John Dawson: **Pages Fourteen and Fifteen:** John Dawson; **Pages Sixteen and Seventeen:** John Dawson; **Bottom,** Karl Edwards; **Pages Twenty and Twenty-one;** John Dawson; **Page Twenty-two:** Walter Stuart; **Page Twenty-three:** Walter Stuart.

Photographic Credits

Cover: Rod Williams *(Bruce Coleman, Inc.);* **Pages Eighteen and Nineteen:** Tom McHugh *(Photo Researchers);* **Page Twenty-two:** David Smith.

Our Thanks To: Erik Eckholm *(Natural History Magazine);* April Bohannan *(National Wildlife Federation);* Pauline Hollmann *(Library of Congress):* Dr. Oliver Ryder *(San Diego Zoo);* Mary Byrd *(Research Department, San Diego Zoo);* Dr. James Dolan *(San Diego Zoo);* Nancy Scott *(Fine Arts Store, San Diego);* Tom Sandler *(The Frame Station, San Diego);* Med Beauregard *(Professional Photographic Services, San Diego);* Lynnette Wexo.

This book is dedicated to Dr. Charles R. Schroeder, a great leader and innovator in the effort to save endagered species.

Creative Education would like to thank Wildflife Education, Ltd., for granting them the rights to print and distribute this hardbound edition.

Contents

Endangered animals are animal species that need our help. For one reason or another, they are having trouble staying alive in their natural homes. Some of them are in so much trouble that scientists have made a list of them called the Endangered Species List—to let everybody know which animals need the most help.

On the following pages of this book, we will be showing you animals that are already on this list. And we will show you the reasons why they are endangered. Unless something is done *very soon* to help these animals, many of them will die out. They will become extinct (X-TINKED).

On these two pages, we want to show you some animals that are not yet on the Endangered Species List—but which could find themselves on the list in the future if people do not change their ways. These are some of the animals that people love the most...but people may cause all of them to become extinct.

SNOWY OWL
Nyctea scandiaca

SCARLET MACAW
Ara macao

RETICULATED GIRAFFE
Giraffa camelopardalis

COUNT RAGGI'S BIRD
OF PARADISE
Paradisaea raggiana

EMPEROR PENGUIN
Aptenodytes forsteri

PEACOCK
Pavo cristatus

BOTTLENOSE
DOLPHIN
Tursiops truncatus

MOUSTACHED
MONKEY
*Cercopithecus
cephus*

WESTERN TRAPOGAN
Trapogan temmincki

WOLF
Canis lupus

KOALA
Phascolarctos cinereus

PYGMY CHIMPANZEE
Pan paniscus

BLACK SWAN
Cygnus atratus

RAINBOW-BILLED TOUCAN
Ramphastos sulfuratus

RED-BILLED TOUCAN
Ramphastos tucanus

RED KANGAROO
Macropus rufus

POLAR BEAR
Thalarctos maritimus

FRILLED LIZARD
Chlamydosaurus sp.

LEOPARD
Panthera pardus

WOOD DUCK
Aix sponsa

7

Why do we need animals and plants?

For one thing, the world would be less beautiful and wonderful without them. Every time an animal or a plant becomes extinct, some beauty and wonder goes out of this world — and we are all poorer for it.

But even more important, all of the animals and plants on earth are *linked together*. Every single species of animal and plant has a special role to play in keeping the world of nature going. Every species depends on other species, and other species depend on it. So every time you take a species away, the natural world does not work quite as well as it used to.

Imagine that the world of nature is like a pyramid made of blocks. Each block has a role to play in holding the pyramid up. If you remove one block, it probably won't make much difference. And even if you remove 25 blocks, it may not cause much damage. But if you remove hundreds and thousands of blocks, the pyramid will almost certainly fall down.

That is the way it is with species. If we remove too many of them, we may find ourselves living one day in a world that doesn't work anymore.

Plants are the basic source of food on earth. They turn sunlight and minerals from the soil into food for animals. One scientist has estimated that every plant species has between 10 and 30 species of living things that depend on it totally for their food. So every time a plant species becomes extinct, ten to thirty other species are lost as well.

8

People are at the top of the pyramid. They often don't realize how much their own survival depends on the survival of other species. But if the pyramid falls, people will fall with it.

How many blocks can we pull out before the pyramid falls down? Nobody really knows. Scientists don't understand the complicated links between various species well enough to be sure. But we can be sure of one thing—if we keep pulling blocks out, we *are* going to suffer for it.

Many animals eat plants, and these animals in turn provide food for the animals that eat meat. If the plant-eaters can't find enough food, or if they die out for other reasons, the meat-eaters will also become extinct.

Insects help plants to reproduce by pollinating them. They are also a major source of food for birds and small mammals. If many insects are lost, the other species that depend on them would also die out.

Animals need homes, just like people do. They need places to live and places to find food. They need places to raise their young in safety. The home of an animal is called its habitat — and the loss of habitat is the most serious threat that many animals face today.

People are destroying animal habitats at an alarming rate. The number of people on earth is growing very fast. As a result, we need more farms to grow food and more room to build houses. So we are taking a lot of land away from animals. Every day, the homes of thousands of animals are destroyed.

Most animals can't find new homes. If their habitats are destroyed, they are destroyed. So if we want to save the animals shown on these pages — and many others as well — we must find ways to save their habitats.

JAPANESE CRESTED IBIS
Nipponia nippon

SPANISH LYNX
Felis pardina

PILEATED GIBBON
Hylobates pileatus

WHITE-EARED PHEASANT
Crossoptilon crossoptilon

Animals that live in tropical forests are suffering the most. The trees are being cut down at the rate of *50 acres a minute.*

DRILL
Papio leucophaeus

PYGMY HIPPOPOTAMUS
Choeropsis liberiensis

CENTRAL ASIAN COBRA
Naja oxiana

ST. LUCIA PARROT
Amazona versicolor

WAGLER'S MACAW
Ara caninde

SOUTHERN BALD EAGLE
Haliaeetus leucocephalus leucocephalus

Meat-eating animals, like Bald eagles, often need large areas in which to hunt their food. If too much of their hunting area is taken away, these animals may starve.

RED UAKARI
Cacajao rubicundus

PROBOSCIS MONKEY
Nasalia larvatus

TAHITI LORIKEET
Vini peruviana

ASIAN ELEPHANT
Elephas maximus

GOLDEN LION TAMARIN
Leontopithecus rosalia

GAUR
Bos gaurus

SONORAN PRONGHORN ANTELOPE
Antilocapra americana sonoriensis

CENTRAL AMERICAN TAPIR
Tapirus bairdii

All wild animals need protected places to raise their young. If there is not enough cover, or if people live too close by, some animals may stop having babies.

UTAH PRAIRIE DOG
Cynomys parvidens

GILA MONSTER
Heloderma suspectum

11

Animals need food and water.

But people often do things that make it hard for wild animals to find the food and water they need.

Some people bring farm animals to graze in places where wild animals need the grass. Some people take all the best food out of an area and leave very little for the animals. Others simply push the animals onto poor land, where food is hard to find, so that the people can have the good land.

And most serious of all, some people spread chemicals in the air and water that poison the food that animals must eat.

When people spray poisons on crops to kill insects, the poisons often stay in the soil for a long time. When it rains, the water running off into streams and rivers carries some of the poisons with it. And this often kills fish. Chemicals pumped into streams by factories kill many more fish.

Sometimes, fish are not poisoned enough to kill them. But they carry the poison in their bodies. And when a meat-eater, like a pelican, eats a lot of fish, the combined poison in all of the fish is enough to kill the pelican.

GALAPAGOS TORTOISE
Testudo elephantopus

ASIATIC BUFFALO
Bubalus bubalis

ASIATIC LION
Panthera leo persica

GIANT ANTEATER
Myrmecophaga tridactyla

CALIFORNIA CONDOR
Gymnogyps californianus

GIANT ARMADILLO
Priodontes giganteus

DALMATIAN PELICAN
Pelecanus crispus

SWINHOE'S PHEASANT
Lophura swinhoii

Grazing farm animals can quickly make land unfit for wildlife. Sheep cut the grass down so close to the ground that it often doesn't grow back. Goats eat young trees, and can destroy forests in this way. When the old trees die, there are no new ones left to replace them.

GREAT
INDIAN BUSTARD
Choriotis nigriceps

NORTHERN
SQUARE-LIPPED
RHINOCEROS
Ceratotherium simum cottoni

KOMODO DRAGON
Varanus komodoensis

JACKASS PENGUIN
Spheniscus demersus

HERMIT IBIS
Geronticus ermita

FIJI BANDED IGUANA
Brachylophus fasciatus

DOUC LANGUR
Pygathrix nemaeus

People sometimes hurt wildlife by bringing wild animals into places where they don't belong. The story of the rats and the mongooses and the Hawaiian birds is a good example of this . . .

Before people came to Hawaii, there were no animals that preyed on birds. For this reason, many types of birds could safely build their nests on the ground. But then, people came to Hawaii. Polynesians came in big canoes and white people came in tall sailing ships . . .

There were rats on the ships, and they quickly came ashore. They started eating the eggs of the ground-nesting birds. People thought they could help the birds by bringing in mongooses to eat the rats . . .

But the people picked the wrong animals. The mongooses did not eat the rats, they ate *the bird eggs*. So thanks to people, the birds now had *two* deadly new enemies . . .

13

A beautiful skin or an unusual pair of horns can be dangerous for the animal that has them. Because there are some people who will pay a lot of money to get them. The best way for us to save the animals shown on these pages—and many other animals—is to get people in rich countries to stop buying products made from wild animals.

Some animals are made into fancy things for people who like to show off. Should pythons and other beautiful snakes be made into belts and boots? Should rare zebras be made into wall decorations?

Parts of animals are turned into useless jewelry and carvings. Do we want to lose more than 100 thousand elephants a year so that people can have these things?

BIGHORN SHEEP
Ovis canadensis

RESPLENDENT QUETZAL
Pharomachrus mocinno

GREVY'S ZEBRA
Equus grevyi

SIBERIAN TIGER
Panthera tigris altaica

INDIAN OR BURMESE PYTHON
Python molurus

JAVAN RHINOCEROS
Rhinoceros sondaicus

Some animals are hunted because they are already very rare. This makes some people want them as trophies, to hang on the wall.

A few animals are endangered because people think that parts of their bodies have magic powers. Some people grind the horns of rhinos into a powder that they say can cure high fevers. Rhino horn sells for 6 thousand dollars a *pound*.

Often, animals are put in danger to get products that can easily be taken from other sources. Do we really want to turn thousands of whales into fertilizer and dog food?

Some selfish people think it is more important to be "elegant" than it is to have beautiful living animals in this world. People like this will pay 200 thousand dollars for a Snow leopard coat.

HUMPBACK WHALE
Megaptera novaeangliae

AFRICAN ELEPHANT
Loxodonta africana

GIANT OTTER
Pteronura brasiliensis

SNOW LEOPARD
Panthera uncia

HELMETED
HORNBILL
Rhinoplax vigil

MOUNTAIN GORILLA
Gorilla gorilla beringei

HAWKSBILL TURTLE
Eretmochelys imbricata

GHARIAL (INDIAN GAVIAL)
Gavialis gangeticus

People who want unusual pets

may sometimes help to push animals closer to extinction, without meaning to do it. They often don't realize that many of the most beautiful and unusual animals in pet stores have been taken from the wild.

LEAR'S MACAW
Anodorhynchus leari

PHILIPPINE EAGLE
Pithecophaga jefferyi

GOLDEN-SHOULDERED PARAKEET
Psephotus chrysopterygius

GOLDEN PARAKEET
Aratinga guarouba

HOODED PARAKEET
Psephotus chrysopterygius

ULTRAMARINE LORIKEET
Vini ultramarina

Every year, more than 7 million wild birds are trapped and sold. Huge areas of tropical forests that were once filled with birds are now almost empty.

LONG-WATTLED UMBRELLABIRD
Cephalopterus penduliger

COTTON-TOP TAMARIN
Saguinus oedipus oedipus

People who trap animals and sell them are only doing it for the money. If everybody stopped buying wild animals, the trappers wouldn't catch them anymore. The animals could stay where they belong—in the wild.

GUAYAQUIL GREAT GREEN MACAW
Ara ambigua guayaquilensis

Parrots are very popular as pets. If people knew what wild parrots must go through on their way to the pet store, they would probably never buy one.

In the wild, the birds are caught in nets, often hundreds at a time. The shock of being caught usually kills 2 out of every 5 birds.

Then the parrots are jammed into tiny cages to be carried to market. They may stay in these cages for days, without enough food and without decent care. At least one out of every 5 birds dies from crowding and lack of food.

SPLENDID PARAKEET
Neophema splendida

THICK-BILLED PARROT
Rhynchopsitta pachyrhyncha pachyrhyncha

ST. VINCENT PARROT
Amazona guildingii

PHILIPPINE TARSIER
Tarsius syrichta

MIKADO PHEASANT
Syrmaticus mikado

SPIX'S MACAW
Cyanopsitta spixii

BORNEAN ORANGUTAN
Pongo pygmaeus

RED-TAILED PARROT
Amazona brasiliensis

GREY-NECKED PICATHARTES
Picathartes oreas

In general, wild animals do not make good pets. They are not tame enough, and they may do things that annoy people. Macaws, for example, like to get up early in the morning and make very loud noises.

Pet stores sell many animals that have not been taken from the wild. These animals were born and raised to be pets. If people buy only these animals, they will have wonderful pets—and they won't be hurting wild animals.

Many parrots can be brought into this country legally. But it is against the law to bring in some species—so they are usually smuggled across the border.

To keep the parrots quiet while they are being smuggled, their beaks are often taped shut. Their feet may be tied together, and they may be stuffed into sacks or wrapped tightly in newspaper. Many of them die from lack of air and rough handling.

In the end, for every beautiful parrot that sits in somebody's living room, at least four others may have been lost along the way.

This rare California Condor is a member of the American Vulture family. At this writing there are only 27 of these birds in existence—both in the wild and in captivity. The California Condor is well known for its powerful and graceful flight and can soar to great heights. Unfortunately, this bird has so far been unable to soar beyond the careless and threatening actions of people. Thus, their numbers dwindle as this beautiful creature is pushed to the brink of extinction.

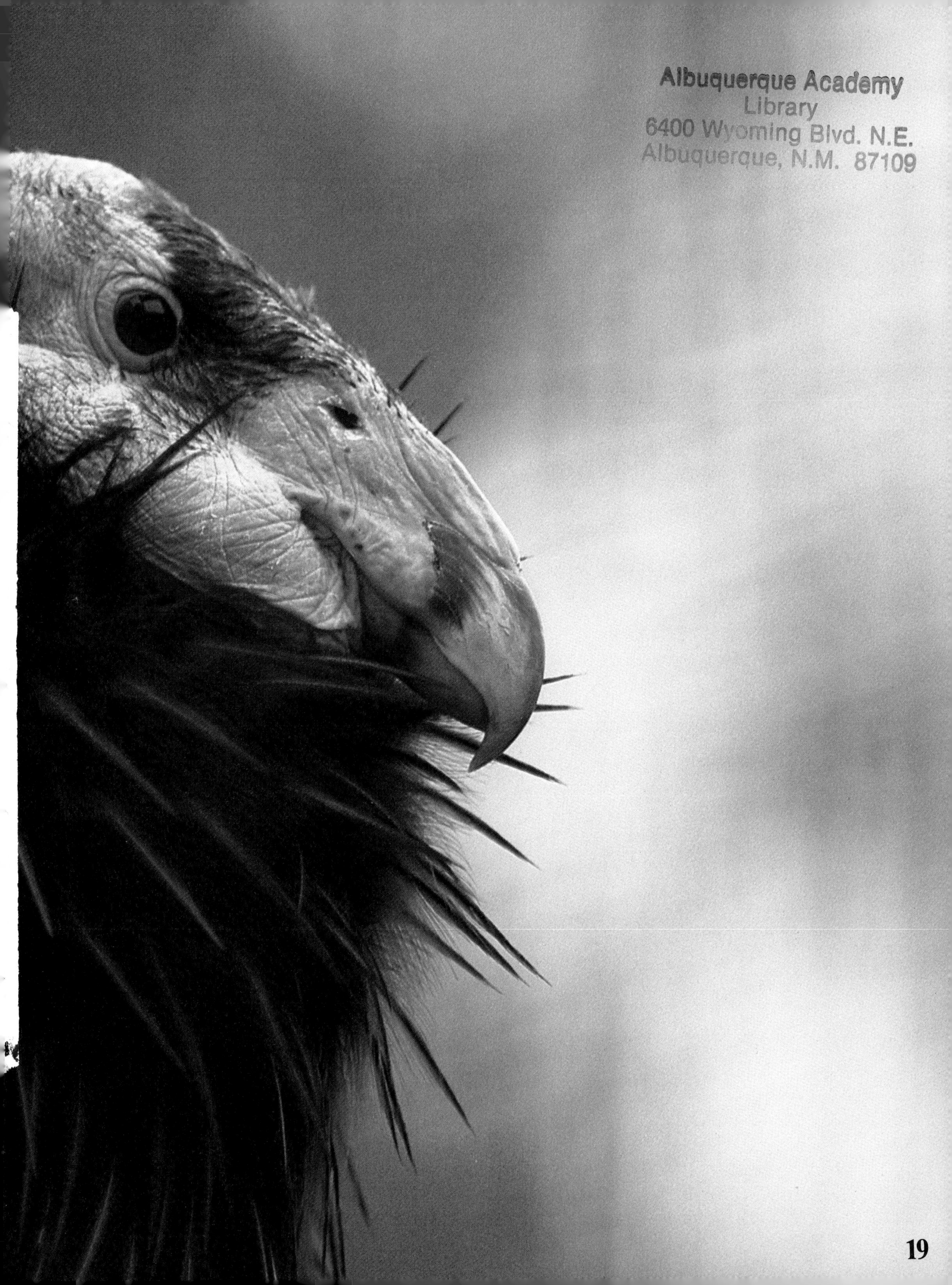

We can save animals if we really want to. The animals at the bottom of these pages are living proof that we can. All of them were headed for extinction when people stepped in to save them.

Some of them were saved by making sure that nobody hunted or trapped them. All of them were given safe homes in zoos and animal preserves. And scientists have worked to help them increase the number of babies they have, to make their numbers grow.

The animals in the picture frames are sad reminders of what can happen if we don't work to save animals. All of them are gone *forever*.

AUROCHS
Bos primigenius

QUAGGA
Equus quagga

GREAT AUK
Alca impennis

PINK-HEADED DUCK
Rhodonessa caryophyllacea

WHITE-TAILED GNU
Connochaetes gnou
More than 4,000 are alive in South Africa.

BONTEBOK
Damaliscus dorcas dorcas

Fifty years ago, fewer than 100 of these antelope were living in Africa. Now there are 1,000.

MONGOLIAN WILD HORSE
Equus przewalskii

Extinct in the wild, these beautiful horses have been kept alive in zoos. There are now over 400 of them in zoos around the world.

STELLER'S SEA COW
Hydrodamalis stelleri

PASSENGER PIGEON
Ectopistes migratorius

DODO
Raphus cucullatus

NEXT?

MOA
Dinornis maximus

AMERICAN BISON
Bison bison

In 1903, fewer than 1,000 survived. There are now more than 80 thousand.

ARABIAN ORYX
Oryx leucoryx

Extinct in the wild, but more than 300 are living in zoos.

GIANT PANDA
Ailuropoda melanoleuca

Protected from habitat destruction by a large preserve in China.

AMERICAN ALLIGATOR
Alligator mississippiensis

A big success. More than 800 thousand now living in the United States.

WHOOPING CRANE
Grus americana

Forty years ago, there were only 21 of these magnificent birds alive. Now there are about 100.

You can help. As you have seen in this book, animals and plants are endangered because of the things that people are doing. Many people have attitudes toward nature that are selfish and destructive. For this reason, the *only* way we can save endangered species is to get people to *change* some of their attitudes.

You can help to make this happen. On these pages, we've listed things that you can do.

Learn as much as you can about nature. Find out everything you can about animals, plants, and the way that nature works. Read books and magazines. Watch television shows about nature. Go to zoos and animal parks to see animals and learn about them. The more you know, the more effective you will be when you try to help.

Write letters and let people know what you think should be done to save endangered species. Write to people who have the power to do something about the problem—the President of the United States, members of Congress, presidents of big companies, mayors of cities. People *do* pay attention to the letters they get. And if they get enough of them, they often do something to help.

Help other people to learn about endangered species—and the reasons why they are endangered. Most people don't realize that they may be part of the reason why animals are in danger. When they find out that their behavior may be hurting animals, many people will try to do better.

Don't buy animals that have been taken from the wild. Every time somebody buys a wild animal in a pet store, this encourages trappers to catch more. When you want a pet, be sure that the animal has been raised in captivity. Ask the people at the pet store to show proof that it has been.

Don't buy products that are made of wild animals. If people do not buy these things, the people who hunt and trap wild animals would have no more reason to do it—there would be no money in it. If you have any doubt about what something is made of and where it comes from, ask the people at the store to tell you.

Support zoos that are breeding endangered species. As you have seen in this book, there are some animals that are only alive today because zoos have protected them and helped them to increase their numbers. Scientists at some zoos are trying to find ways to save many more endangered animals. Join a zoo in your area, and ask them what you can do to help.

Support organizations that are working locally and worldwide to save endangered species. There are many things you can do on your own to help, but a group of people working together has greater power to get things done. We have listed some of the leading organizations on these pages. Get in touch with them, and ask them to tell you more about what they do. They will welcome your interest.

American Association
of Zoological Parks & Aquariums
Oglebay Park
Wheeling, West Virginia 26003

Canadian Nature Federation
Suite 203, 75 Albert Street
Ottawa, Ontario K1P 6G1
Canada

Canadian Wildlife Federation
1673 Carling Avenue
Ottawa, Ontario K2A 1C4
Canada

Defenders of Wildlife
1244 Nineteenth Street, N.W.
Washington, D. C. 20036

Elsa Wild Animal Appeal
P. O. Box 4572
North Hollywood, California 91607

Environmental Defense Fund
444 Park Avenue South
New York, New York 10016

Friends of the Earth International
1045 Sansome Street
San Francisco, California 94111

Center for the Reproduction
of Endangered Species
P. O. Box 551
San Diego, California 92112

Going...

The growing number of people on earth is the main cause for all of the problems shown in this book. As the human population continues to grow, there is a greater and greater demand for living space, food, lumber, minerals, and other things that must be taken from nature. Two hundred years ago, there were fewer than one billion people on earth. There was plenty of food and living space for both people and animals. Today, there are over 4½ billion people on earth, and things are getting tight. In the future, if the number of humans continues to grow, there won't be any more food and room for animals.

Going...   Going...   Gone?

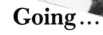

Index